NATIONAL ARCHAEOLOGICAL MUSEUM OF ATHENS

TRANSLATION:
LIZA MANTZOPOULOU

NATIONAL ARCHAEOLOGICAL MUSEUM

TEXT
BY ANAST. P. VARVARRIGOS
DPL. LETTERS - ARCHAEOLOGIST

ATHENS 1976

PRINTED IN GREECE BY VOUTSAS BROTHERS

NATIONAL ARCHAEOLOGICAL MUSEUM

THE NATIONAL ARCHAEOLOGICAL MUSEUM AND ITS HISTORY

It is now a fact that, in the last few years, Greece has actually become an attraction pole for tourists. Thousands of people from all over the world start from some far-off country and come here, asking to get acquainted with the source of the Greek ancient civilization. Greece, with its innumerable archaeological finds and its natural beauties, grants the visitor unforgetable memories — something to remember long after his journey is over...

And after the tourist has finished with the open-air archaeological sites, he asks to visit the housed treasures as well, which, together with the open-air archaeological monuments, attest to the grandeur of the Greek race. Such treasures are kept in the Greek museums which house the best of what the chisel of the ancient artist has made.

There are more than eighty museums all over the country, where the result of the human labour and art are exhibited, from the very ancient years down to our own days. Of all eighty museums, the largest and the richest in archaeological exhibits is the National Archaeological Museum, located in Athens at Patission street, just between Ipirou and Tositsa streets.

The foundations of the National Archaeological Museum were laid in the year 1866 on a large site donated to the Greek State by Helen Tositsas. With his generous offer of 250,000 drachmae, Dem. Bernadakis from Petroupolis contributed to the construction of the Museum. Later on, namely in 1874, with the Greek State's financial assistance, the western side of the Museum was completed.

In the days of Charilaos Trikoupis, the Greek politician known for his love for archaeology, the Museum, called until then "Central Museum", was officially named "National Archaeological Museum" (Royal Decree 19/4/1881).

The Museum was built according to the design of the architect Ludwig Lange. Its construction was completed in the year 1889, after certain modifications that Ernst Ziller, known for his architectural attainments in Greece, brought on the original design of Lange. The modifications were actually made on the eastern wing, the central hall and, particularly, on the facade of the building.

The transfer of the archaeological finds to the newly-built Museum was made in 1891. The first exhibition of the archaeological treasures in the halls of the Museum is due to the great interest and the painstaking efforts of the memorable archaeologists Panagiotis Kavvadias and Christos Tsountas.

The worst enemy of museums the world all over is war. So, the Greek-Italian War, which broke out in the year 1940, caused the destruction of a great deal of exhibits which had to be packed in boxes, while many statues had to be buried to avoid destructive bombing raids.

After the end of the war, the building of the National Archaeological Museum was subjected to certain modifications. After a close co-operation between the architect P. Karadinos and Chr. Karouzos, the memorable Director of the Museum, the old building was modified, without violations whatever on the original design of the architects Lange and Ziller.

To-day, the National Archaeological Museum is the pride of Greece. It avails of a highly specialized scientific and technical staff which can make the best possible use of what so many centuries and eras have treasured. The valuable remnants have been aesthetically placed in the spacious and well-lit 35 halls of the Museum.

EXHIBITS AND ERAS

The National Archaeological Museum is really unique in its kind. The rich collection of the exquisite exhibits it houses, and still the sensational way the latter are exposed, enable the visitor to follow the evolution of Greek Art — from the very early years of its birth in the Neolithic Age right down to the years of the Roman occupation.

THE NEOLITHIC CIVILIZATION

The Neolithic civilization is the first civilization to appear in Greece. It actually started about 7000 B.C. and lasted until 2700 B.C. The Neolithic Age is divided into three periods, namely: a) the Early Neolithic period, b) the Middle Neolithic period, and c) the Late Neolithic period.

When we refer to the Neolithic Age, we actually mean a cultural and economic stage mainly characterized by the practice of agriculture and livestock breeding.

The several finds unearthed in this connection disclose that, in the Neolithic period a systematic cultivation of the land had started, while people were already making their permanent settlements. Apart from stone tools, the people of that time also made vases of clay, varying in size and form and bearing most characteristic decoration. They made, in addition, stone weapons and a wide range of stone or clay idols, that is statuettes mostly portraying female and rarely male figures.

Such Neolithic statuettes were made by the inhabitants of rural settlements and were of a ritual character. The female figures symbolized fertility, and this is exactly why they are shown with well-grown breasts, a well-marked belly and buttocks.

The first to make a systematic study of the Neolithic era was the pioneering Greek archaeologist Christos Tsountas. In the district of Thessaly, the archaeologist's spade brought to light two famous Neolithic settlements, Dimini and Sesklo.

CYCLADIC CIVILIZATION

In addition to the Neolithic civilization of Mainland Greece, another equally important civilization develops in the Cyclades. The new civilization, called Cycladic after the place where it was born, coincides chronologically with the early Bronze Age.

The development of the Cycladic civilization was favoured by such climatological conditions as the mild climate of the Cyclades group. The artistic nature of the inhabitants of the Cyclades, together with the abundant marble of the island of Naxos and Paros, and the obsidian of Melos, contributed effectively to the development of the Cycladic civilization.

The Cycladic civilization is sub-divided into three phases, namely: a) 2700-2400 B.C., b) 2400-2200 B.C., and c) 2200-2000 B.C.

In the course of those three periods of the Cycladic civilization, the art of ceramics actually develops. We meet masterfully made marble and clay idols, vases, etc. Among the exquisite marble idols exhibited in the Cycladic collection of the National Archaeological Museum we might single out a seated male figure playing the harp (fig. 1).

The statuette is characterized by a striking abstraction and a strict simplicity of line confined to the mere depiction of the form. It seems that the artists of the Cyclades, apart from the sensitivity and the craftmanship characterizing them, also possessed an intelligent conception of the volume. The maker of this wonderful statuette has made the most of the curves formed by the movement of the body and the harp, as the latter stands on the player's lap.

In this masterpiece of the Early Cycladic period, the visitor of the Museum will easily discern the artistic nature of the craftsman, long experience and an insistent effort.

THE MYCENAEAN CIVILIZATION

By Mycenaean civilization we mean the civilization which, starting from Mycenae from which it has also taken its name, spread nearly over the whole of the Mediterranean basin and dominated over the place for the long period of five centuries (1600 B.C. - 1100 B.C.). The Mycenaean era, also called Late Helladic, is divided into three sub-periods, namely: Mycenaean I, II, III. The adopted term Mycenaean is not incidental or casual — it merely assures the importance of the place which, as the Homeric epic puts it, was "rich in gold". Mycenae was the seat of the dynasty of Atreides.

Our reconnaissance with the Mycenaean civilization is mainly due to excavations carried out at Mycenae by Heinrich Schliemann. Relying on an account given by the ancient Baedeker, Pausanias, Schliemann started uncovering in the year 1876 the famous shaft graves in the Grave Circle A', behind the Lion Gate. In these graves, the fabulous Mycenaean Treasures were found. In the Mycenaean hall of the National Archaeological Museum, which is actually the trunk of the whole structure, we can admire, tastefully placed in glass show-cases, the best of the Mycenaean works of art, an art which starts with the mason who hewed and laid the large boulders used in the Cyclopean walls and closes with the gifted makers of the gold funerary items contained in the tombs. These valuable articles are ornaments buried with the dead and are mostly made of massive gold. Among them there are gold masks, diadems, gold rings and earrings, sword hilts, gold sheets, and so many other articles, all of superb artistry. One of the gold masks exposed in the "Mycenaean" room of the Museum (fig. 3) was found in shaft grave V and dates about 1600 B.C.

The Mycenaean goldsmith has so skilfully reproduced the dead king's features on the soft gold. Looking at the gold deathmasks in the Mycenaean hall, the modern visitor's thought is carried far, too far, thousands of years back to the Argolid Plain and to the fatal House of the Atreides, the mighty dynasty pursued by overwhelming misfortunes.

Equally impressive are the daggers which can hardly escape the visitor's attention (fig. 7). They come from the royal tomb V of ancient Mycenae. These daggers were surely held by the strong hands of the Homeric sovereigns who, together with their people, created a perfect civilization, a civilization dominated by the spirit of contest, which was the main characteristic of the Achaeans' life. And this spirit of contest is something that the visitor of the Museum can easily discern by observing the decorations of the daggers. Vivid scenes of chase are portrayed on the daggers, while Mycenaeans armed with shields, arrows and spears seem to be engaged in lion hunting.

The people of Mycenaean Greece attained an impressive progress by the years, while the several small states they established grew into important centres of the Mycenaean civilization. The inhabitants of the Mycenaean centres made particular progress in trade. Their works of art reached as far as Spain and even the Balearic Islands.

GEOMETRIC PERIOD

By Geometric period we mean that period of art which started in Greece with the Dorians' invasion in 1100 B.C.

As already known, the Dorians' sway ruined the best of what the Mycenaean civilization had created. With the arrival of the Dorians in Greece art actually stops and, according to the opinion of many art historians, is succeeded by the obscure years of the Dorian occupation. None can naturally doubt the fact that, with the Dorians, art did stop. We should not forget, however, that the traveller can stop for a while, just to rest and gather new, refreshed vigour before he goes on with his journey. And, then, let's not forget that each dark age may be the beginning of a golden era.

POTTERY OF THE GEOMETRIC PERIOD

We can note that, in the course of the 10th century B.C., the inhabitants of Greece start to manifest some artistic tendency evidenced in the works they make. The vases, for example, disclose faint efforts for an external decoration of some kind. Pottery painters are now taking their first hesitant steps. In their start, however, there is a restrictive rule they have to observe: they avoid to use a free hand, which they have to replace by the ruler and compass, which are purely geometric instruments.

It is easily understood, therefore, that all the motifs were of a geometric form. And this is exactly the reason why the art period starting with the 10th century B.C. is known as the Geometric Period.

The motifs used in the Geometric period to decorate the pottery are mainly straight, parallel or bent lines, meanders, zigzags, etc.

The pottery style of the 10th century B.C. is also called Protogeometric. In the National Archaeological Museum, 8th century is represented by the funerary Amphora of Dipylon (fig. II).

An amphora is a vase with two handles, one on each side, and both on the same level. The Amphora of Dipylon is a tomb amphora, found at Dipylon and dated about 750 B.C.

It is a work of the now mature Geometric style. It is 1.50 m. high and the main scene is confined to the handle-zone of the vase.

The subject depicted here is the "prothesis" (lying-in-state) of the dead. Lying on the funeral bier is the dead. On both sides of the bier, the relatives stand mourning the dead with their hands placed on their heads, according to the customs prevailing at that time.

The artist seems to dislike empty space, that is he is possessed by the "horror vacui". This is the reason why he tends to decorate the vase all over.

On the neck of the vase there are grazing fawns, while on the remaining surface there is nearly the entire repertory of the geometric motifs.

WORKS OF SCULPTURE

The first half of the 7th century B.C. is a real milestone in the ancient Greek sculpture. The works of that era make, with their imposing size, the Daedalic prelude in the Greek sculpture.

THE KOUROI OF THE ARCHAIC ERA

The Archaic era was a preliminary stage which made the indispensible precursor of the Classical era, in the course of which Greek civilization, and particularly Greek art, reached its apogee. During the Archaic era, apart from the advanced architectural and pottery art, we also have a certain progress of sculpture. This is the first time that life-size statues are made.

It is generally noted that, in the ancient years, the phenomenon of death held people in awe. And this is the reason why, in every era, some artists seem to be mainly engaged in the creation of works of art closely related with the event of death.

It is also known that, in ancient years the dead were considered to be something sacred, treated for that with all due honours and lavish care from the part of the living, who meant to express, in this way, their belief in after-life.

The dead's relatives, however, did not only care for the interior of the tomb (which they decorated with the several offerings they laid in it), they also adorned the exterior of it. For that purpose they set up on the tomb plaques (the so-called tomb stelae serving as a "sign" or marker), huge vases and, particularly, funerary over life-size statues.

These statues, most frequently made in the Archaic era, were used to denote young boys and girls. They are shown erect, rather immobile, completely nude, of an athletic look and with a characteristic stiffness of the limbs. The male figures were called K o u r o i, while the females, usually shown wearing their finest apparel, were called K o r a i.

Among the oldest Kouroi of the Archaic era exposed in the National Archaeological Museum is the K o u r o s o f S o u n i o n (fig. 12).

He was found at Sounion in 1906 and is datable about 610 B.C. The Kouros is over life-size (namely 3.05 m. high) and curved in coarse-grained marble. He has long hair, closed almond-shaped eyes, while his sealed lips seem to imply a certain smile, the so-called "archaic smile".

As it is also the case with the other archaic Kouroi, the technique of the Kouros of Sounion reminds of the characteristic technique of the Egyptian statues, with the only difference that the former develops rapidly and becomes more livelier and more supple-limbed, in less than one hundred years from the time the first Kouros appeared.

But, within one hundred years, sculpture produced another Kouros, differring completely from the Kouros of Sounion in body structural details. The new Kouros is the Kouros of Melos (fig. 14). It is datable to 550 B.C. and was found on the island of Melos. On this statue the transition to a more naturalistic technique is actually evident.

Contrary to the Kouros of Sounion, the Kouros of Melos is not over life-size, and his body is characterized by a natural slenderness. The "archaic smile" is more expressive, while the whole stance suggests more sense of life. The hands are still locked to the sides of the body, which is characteristic of the archaic rigidity. The rich wavy hair falls down over the shoulders and it is artfully kept back with a band. Natural supple curves outline the body.

The Kouros of Volomandra (fig. 16-17), appearing ten years after the Kouros of Melos, persuades the onlooker that art is not static, but it is something continually developing.

The Kouros of Volomandra is among the charming statues of the National Archaeological Museum. It dates from about 540 B.C. and was found at the place Kalyvia (Mesogeia, Attica). He is of natural height and, like the other Kouroi, he has the left foot brought forward. His hands are still hanging down along-side the body, but they seem to be ready to bend.

The sculptor has given the marble a wonderful finish. The refined features and, above all, the smile of the Kouros is something to draw the attention and the admiration of the onlooker. The projecting breast gives the impression that this is a living creature just breathing.

We can therefore say, as the memorable Al. Philadelpheus had characteristically mentioned, that one can discern in ancient Greek art this very deep feeling for the good and, still, this faithful reproduction of nature. Those are the two vital elements which the ancient Greek artists have always followed and which have endowed their art with a grace and elegance not to be equalled by any artist of any age or era.

BRONZE STATUES OF THE 6TH AND 5TH CENTURY B.C.

In the National Archaeological Museum bronze workers of the 6th and 5th century B.C. are represented by two exquisite bronze statues: a) the Kouros (or Apollo) of Piraeus, and b) Poseidon of Artemisium.
The Kouros (or Apollo) of Piraeus (fig. 31-32). It is the oldest and unique of its kind bronze statue of the Archaic era. It bears much resemblance to the marble Kouroi of the Archaic era. As, however, the stance of the figure is generally reminiscent of a divine creature, it could be presumed to be a statue of Apollo, probably holding a libation phiale in his right hand.

The plastic structural formation of the body and, above all, the movement of the limbs expressed by the bent arms attest to an art now progressing.

The Kouros (or Apollo) of Piraeus was incidentally found in Piraeus in 1959. The divine stance of the body, together with the serene countenance is something that the visitor cannot help admiring. It was probably made about 525 B.C. by some gifted Athenian bronze worker.

Poseidon of Artemisium (fig. 20-21). The one to visit the Museum to-day is sure to be astounded by the over life-size statue of Poseidon found at Artemisium north of Euboea. The gigantic ruler of seas and oceans appears in the visitor's eyes in all his divine splendour.

Even to this day, the imposing presence of the god reduces the human beings to nothingness, his divine lordly look strikes them with awe. The huge statue asks for an ample space to show off its beauty and this is exactly the reason why it has been placed right in the centre of the room, dominating the other exhibits all around.

The god is presented nude, with his left leg thrust forward and his right toes just touching the ground. The god's countenance is something to thrill the present-day visitor. And those empty sockets would have surely contained the fiery eyes with which the majestic looking god would scrutinize his vast realm of waters.

With his right bent hand, the god was probably brandishing his trident, the shaft of which was passing through the open fingers right in front of the face. The nude body shows that the bronze god has just come out of the foamy waves he rules over.

Poseidon of Artemisium is probably the work of the famous bronze-worker Kalamis and it is chronologically placed between 460 and 450 B.C.

GRAVE STELAE OF THE 5TH CENTURY B.C.

The great classical era is in its glory in the 5th century B.C. In the course of the 5th century nearly all art expressions continue their steady development. Concurrently, tomb reliefs exhibit an impressive expansion.

Goethe himself, deeply moved by the significance of the Greek tomb stelae, has written: "It is a rose-scented breeze that reaches us from the tombs of the ancient Greeks. The monuments are warm and moving always portraying life. The artist depicts the mere presence of the persons, thus carrying on their existance to eternity".

Among the most famous grave stelae of the National Archaeological Museum is the Grave Stele of Hegeso (fig. 24).

This stele is a naiskos crowned by a pediment. It was set up on the tomb of Hegeso, the young daughter of Proxenos, as it is proved by the inscription on the top "ΗΓΗΣΩ ΠΡΟΞΕΝΟ".

Hegeso is depicted comfortably seated on a turned chair. She is dressed in a thin chiton and a himation, while the grieved face is enveloped in a mourning head-cover. A deep grief is diffused on her face for her premature death, while the sealed lips seem to suggest a faint bitter smile.

A woman-servant is standing before the deceased lady. The former is wearing a sleeved chiton, an evidence of her humble descent. She keeps a pyxis (jewel box) open before Hegeso, who is probably taking in her right hand one of her favourite jewels. This gesture may express one of the deceased lady's last desires to enjoy the pleasures of life.

The visitor of the Museum cannot miss the restrained sorrow diffused on the faces of the two women, so artfully made by the chisel of the talented artist. The stele was found at Kerameikos and was made about 410 B.C.

Another funerary relief to move the visitor is the relief of the Young Man and the Servant (fig. 23).

It comes from the upper part of a tomb stele. It presents a dead youth, an ephebe, holding his right hand out in an effort to close a cage. In the left hand he is holding a little bird he has taken out of the cage.

The artist has shown the ephebe casually dressed in a himation falling in rich folds. A cat curled up on the left below seems to wait in vain. The whole picture is supplemented by the small servant-boy standing by, with a look of immense grief over his childish face.

The place where the stele was found is still uncertain. It was made about 430 B.C.

BRONZE STATUES OF THE 4TH CENTURY B.C.

The most representative samples of bronze working in the 4th century are the Ephebe of Anticythera and the Ephebe of Marathon. They are both exquisite pieces of art which cannot miss the visitor's attention.

The Ephebe of Anticythera (fig. 43-44).

The statue was found fragmented, in the year 1900, off the shores of the island of Anticythera. It is over life-size and probably made by some Peloponnesian artist about 340 B.C. It may represent some hero or god, but most probably an athlete. The youth rests the weight of his body on his left leg. His left arm falls limp, while the right hand is raised in a diagonal counterbalance.

Much has been really told about the open fingers. What was the Ephebe holding, we wonder! It was probably a sphere-shaped object.

The strong and well-built torso is supported by the slender legs. The Kouros stands serene, athletic looking, with particularly delicate features. The expression on his face implies a certain shyness characteristic of the youth. He has short curly hair and vivid expressive eyes. The athletic body of the Ephebe is a proof of the favourable effects exercise had on the bodies of the youth in antiquity.

Another masterpiece of bronze work is the Ephebe of Marathon (fig. 29-30). The statue represents a standing young man, resting his light well-exercised body on his left leg. He has raised the right hand, while he keeps his look fixed on some object he was probably holding on his open left palm.

The vivid eyes of this well-preserved statue remind much of the previous Ephebe of Anticythera. The hair of this Kouros, too, is short and curly, while the line of the nose stresses the Greek descent of the Ephebe.

It was found deep in the sea of Marathon in 1925. It is 1.30 m. high and dates from about the middle of the 4th century.

HELLENISTIC ERA

According to the historical sources, the hellenistic period is chronologically placed between 323 and 31 B.C. After the splitting up of the vast empire of Alexander the Great, the states which were created — such as Egypt and Pergamos — became centres not only of Greek culture, but also of Greek art. This art, which starts in 323 B.C. and ends in 31 B.C., was called Hellenistic Art.

The Hellenistic art develops nearly in all sectors in general. The archaeological finds of that era, whether architectural or sculptural, disclose that art in the course of the Hellenistic years did not actually stop — on the contrary, it continued developing assuming a more naturalistic form.

The tendency of the sculptors of the Hellenistic era to make over life-size statues becomes evident in the Poseidon of Melos (fig. 51).

The colossal statue is mounted on a pedestal. Poseidon is presented standing, his head held up, his curly hair in disorder. The austere look makes the onlooker think that the mighty god is scanning the realm of waters he dominates.

The pose of the statue suggests a supernatural vigour, characteristic of the Hellenistic era. The raised right hand was probably holding the trident. The left hand, lowered in a contrasting movement to the right one, is holding the garment artfully covering the lower part of his body. The upright dolphin stuck on the god's right leg was probably intended to prop the statue.

The colossal statue was found on Melos in 1877.

Apart from the colossal statues, the Hellenistic era has to exhibit most beautiful sculptural groups, as the famous statue of Aphrodite, Pan and Eros (fig. 53).

The goddess of love and beauty is shown nude, holding in the right hand her sandal with which she is threatening the goat-footed Pan, who was spying on her taking her bath. The body is slightly bent in a contrasting movement to the closed limbs.

This group of statues makes a magnificent sculptural composition. A little Eros is flying between Aphrodite and Pan trying to reconcile them, something he finally did, because Aphrodite, in spite of her threatening gesture, is now smiling at Pan.

It was found on Delos in 1904. Made early in the 1st century B.C.

It can be generally accepted that all the works of the Greek antiquity appeal to the soul of the present-day visitor, thrilling him through and through. These masterpieces of art will always stand as the unquestionable evidence of a heavy and charished inheritance bequeathed to posterity.

THE ANTIQUITIES OF THERA
(Temporary Exhibition)

Thera, also known as Santorin, is a most peculiar island indeed. The world-wide interest it attracts can be attributed to both, the antiquities lately found in the place, and to the individual and unique colour of the island itself. More than half of the island has been born from its volcano, while the remaining is the residue of an ancient island.

From 3000 B.C. we find the island inhabited by the people of Kares and, very early, it bears the influence of neighbouring Crete. Most unfortunately, however, a terrible earthquake, which shook the island in about 1500 B.C., put an end to the serene life of the inhabitants and plunged half of the island to the ever-shadowed depths of the sea. And, then, left in a queer half-moon shape, Thera remained deserted and sunk into oblivion.

Thera, however, is not the island to be met everywhere — it is a vision, it is a passionate and dramatic image of the human suffering and sacrifice.

In the last few years, the archaeological spade proved that the historical past of Thera was not thoroughly known. And this proof is due to the archaeological finds of the late Professor

Marinatos, the devoted investigator of the prehistoric civilization of Thera. Professor Marinatos carrying out excavations at the southern part of the island — namely near the village Akrotiri — brought to light a vast prehistoric civilization buried, for three and a half thousand years, under layers of pumice and hot lava.

The most important of the prehistoric finds of Thera are now temporarily exhibited on the first floor of the National Archaeological Museum. The visitor will admire here most interesting ceramics and the famous frescoes of Thera showing scenes from the life of the island's prehistoric inhabitants. Of the Theraic frescoes, we could single out the Boxing Boys (fig. 58-59). The gifted artist has portrayed two children, of about 8 to 9 years old, engaged in boxing. From the subject point of view, this is probably the oldest fresco in the history of art.

The body lines of the tender age, so perfect and accurate as they look, make us feel that we do see the children boxing. Their bodies are painted red, their hair ends to two long black plaits and they have their ears and their ankles decorated with luxurious jewels. The artist is probably depicting two little twin princes.

In the same room decorated with the Boxing Boys, the archaeologist's spade uncovered another wall frescoed with the fantastic Antelopes (fig. 64). The artist of 1500 B.C. depicts two antelopes, painted in black lines against a whitish background. The two animals seem to be courting with each other. This is proved by the turned head of the first antelope, by their open mouths and, above all, by their raised tails. The fresco covers the western wall of the room.

Finally, the largest and still the most impressive Theraic fresco exhibited in the National Museum is the Spring fresco (fig. 63). This is the first time that a fresco of the Aegean comes out to light complete, covering the three walls of a room.

The artist depicts a landscape of Thera, as this had been before the fatal volcanic erruption. The picture is dominated by multi-coloured rocks with the characteristic Theraic lilies growing among them. Right above the lilies, swallows wooing and twittering, flying single or coupled, herald in Spring. The fresco dates from about 1500 B.C., extends over the three walls of the room and it is about 14 m^2.

These are but samples of more frescoes which have not been exposed until now. All together, they make the unquestionable evidence of a most ancient civilization which, passing through a long series of centuries, has reached us nearly intact.

Cycladic marble statuette representing a male figure playing the harp. Found at Keros. Between 2700-2000 B.C.

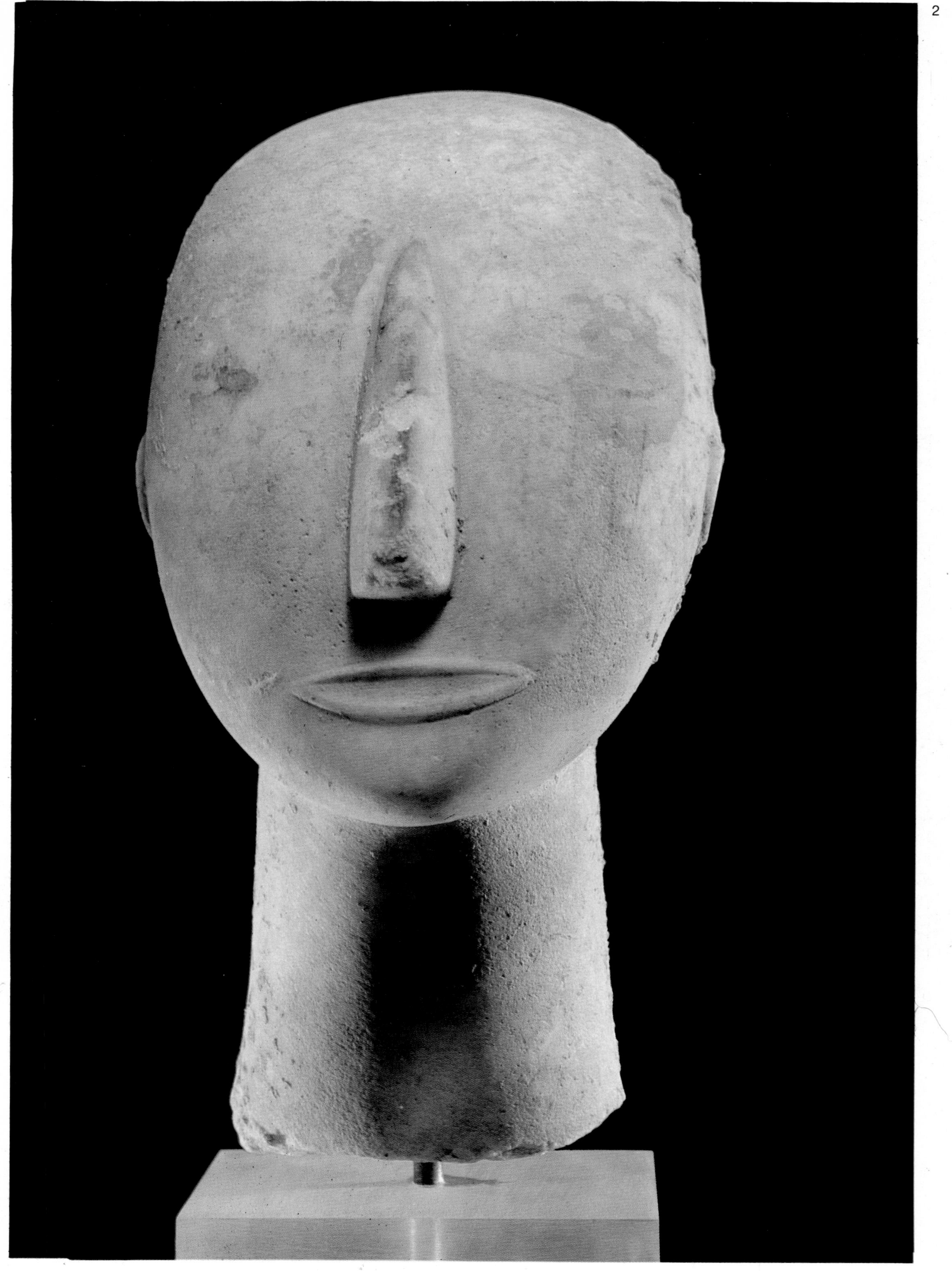

Marble head from Paros dated 2800-2200 B.C. Found at Amorgos.

Gold mask from the royal shaft grave V of Mycenae. 16th cent. B.C.

624·

3

·253· ·259· ·254

4

Three gold masks from the royal grave IV of Mycenae.

Two gold cups found in a tholos tomb at Vapheio in Lakonia. The Mycenaean goldsmith has masterfully depicted the capture of a bull on the first cup, and an idyllic scene with cattle on the second. 15th cent. B.C.

5·

1758·

·6

·1759

Three Mycenaean daggers with inlaid decorations in gold, silver and niello. Mycenaeans armed with shields, arrows and spears are portrayed engaged in lion hunt. 16th cent. B.C.

8

Rhyton of silver in the form of a bull's head, from the grave IV in the Grave Circle A of the Mycenaean citadel. 16th cent. B.C.

Mycenaean citadel. Some archaeologists believe it to be the head of a Sphinx. 13th cent. B.C.

Limestone head of a woman. Found in Grave Circle A on the Mycenaean citadel. Some archaeologists believe it to be the head of a Sphinx. 13th cent. B.C.

9

Fresco from the Palace of Tiryns.

The big amphora from Dipylon, a characteristic sample of the mature geometric style. The subject-matter is the "prothesis" (lying-in-state) of the dead. Dated c. 800 B.C.

11

804

12

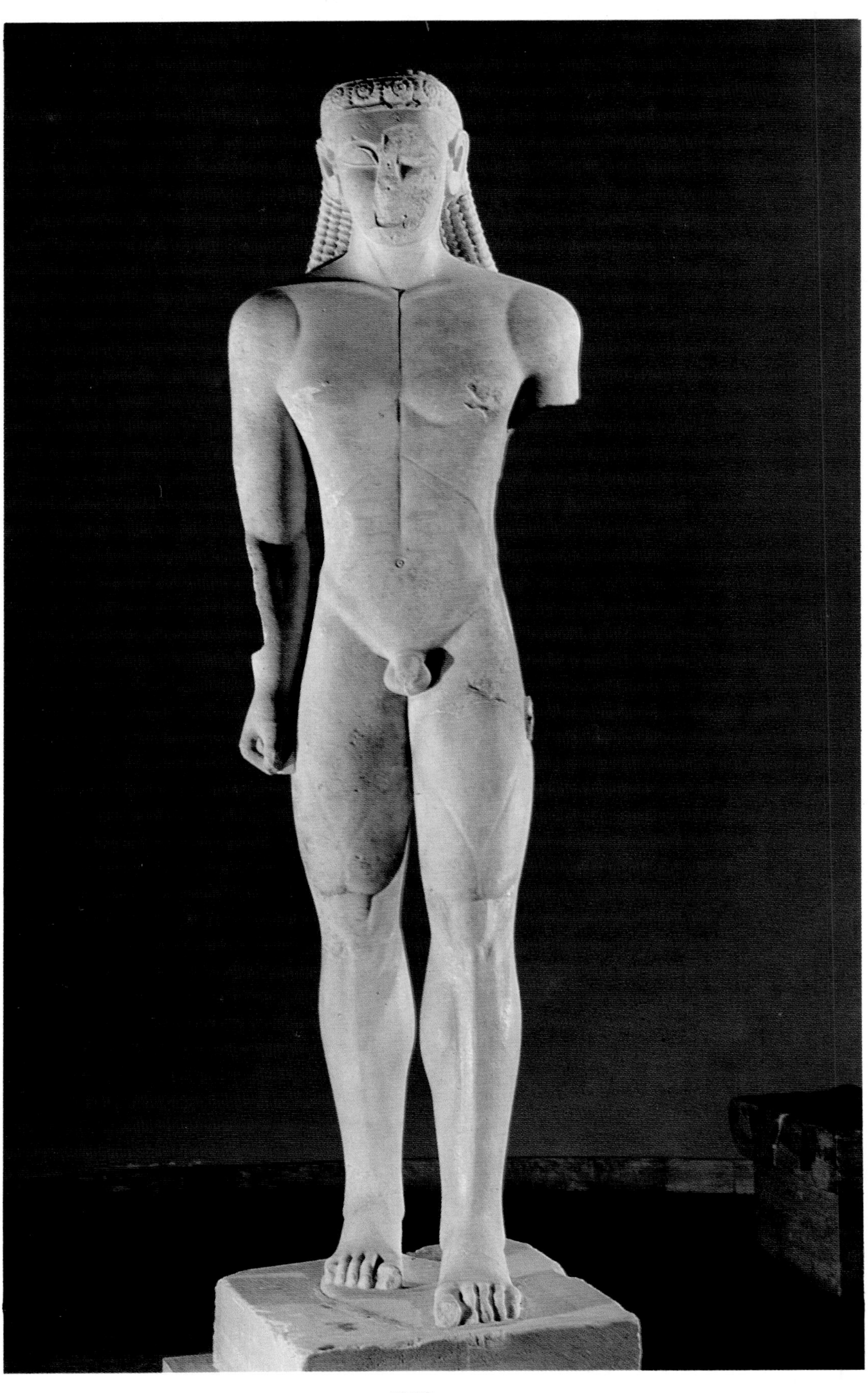

The Kouros of Sounion. Found at Sounion in 1906 and made from coarse-grained Naxian marble in c. 600 B.C.

2720

13

29

The stele of Aristion is, as understood by the inscription on the base, the work of Aristokles. Made between 510-500 B.C.

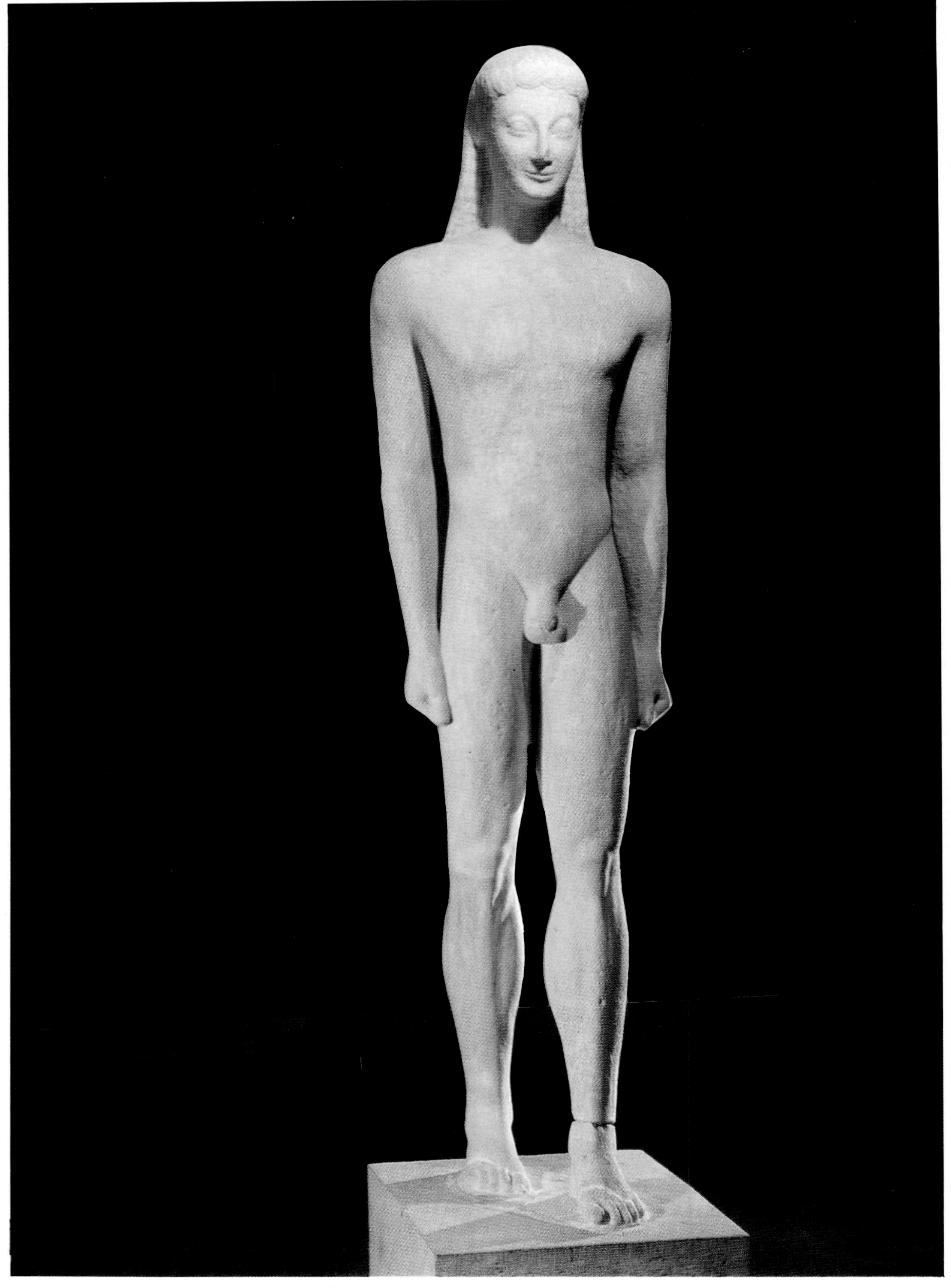

The Kouros of Melos. Found on Melos and dated to c. 550 B.C.

15

The Nike of Delos. Found on the island of Delos and dated to c. 550 B.C.

1906

16-

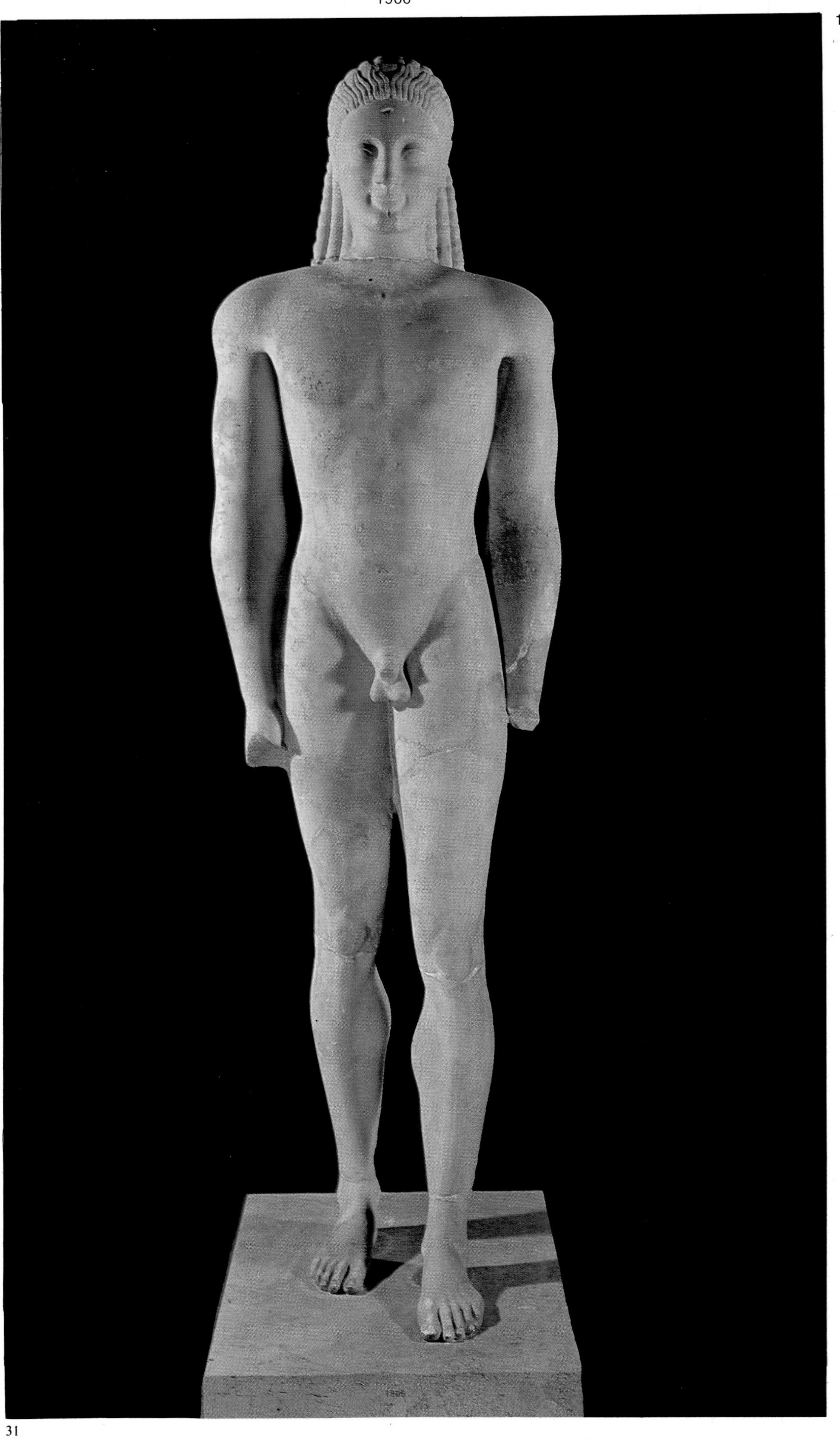

The Kouros of V
omandra, one of
charming statues of
Archaeological
Museum. It was found
Volomandra (Kalyv
of Mesogeia (Attic
Dated to c. 540 B.C.

The Kouros of Volomandra (detail).

18

The Discophoros (discus-bearer) of Dipylon. Fragment from the upper part of a funerary stele depicting an athlete with the discus raised over his head. Found at Dipylon and made in c. 560 B.C.

The Stele of the Running Hoplite. This funerary monument depicts a helmeted young man in the act of running. Dated 510 B.C.

19

1959

The Poseidon of Artemisiu
(detail).

The Poseidon of Artemisium, one of the exquisite bronze statues of the National Archaeological Museum. It was probably made by Kalamis between 470-450 B.C. Found near Cape Artemisium on NE of Euboea.

126

22

The large votive relief of Eleusis representing Demeter, Triptolemos and Persephone. Found at Eleusis.

The grave stele of the Young Man and the Servant. Made in c. 430 B.C.

23

715

3624

The grave stele of Hegeso, daughter of Proxenos, is the noblest Attic grave stele of the Archaeological Museum. Found at Kerameikos and made in c. 410 B.C.

The little Jockey Boy mounted on the horse of Artemisium.

25

The little Jockey Boy of Artemisium. Dated to about the midsecond cent. B.C.

15177

26

The Hermes of Andros represented as the guardian of the dead. (Copy of a Praxitelean work of the 2nd cent. B.C.).

The "Diadoumenos", a marble copy of a bronze statue made by Polykleitos in c. 420 B.C.

28

1826

15118

The Ephebe of Marathon (detail).

The Ephebe of Marathon. Bronze statue found at the bottom of the sea of Marathon and made between 340-330 B.C.

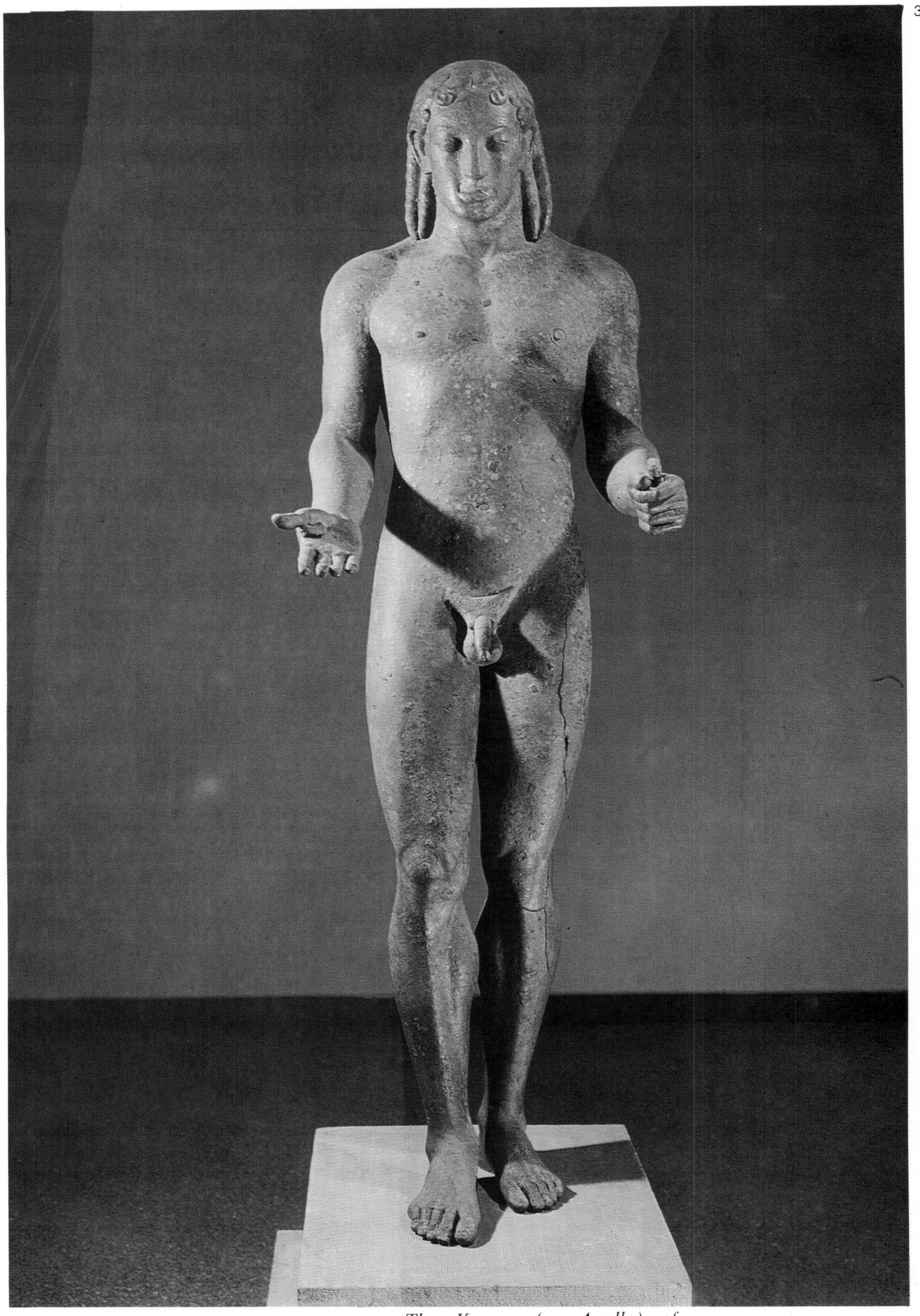

The Kouros (or Apollo) of Piraeus. The earliest bronze statue of the Greek sculpture. Found at Piraeus and made between 530-520 B.C.

The Kouros of Piraeus (detail).

32

*Athena of Piraeus (d-
tail).*

33-34

*Bronze statue of Athena found at
Piraeus. 4th cent. B.C.*

35

6447

Bronze statuette portraying Athena Promachos. 5th cent. B.C.

36

16547

Bronze statuette of a rider. Found at Dodone and dated between 575-560 B.C.

37

6440

Bronze head of Zeus from Olympia. Datable to the 6th cent. B.C.

38

6446

Bronze head of a bearded man.
Made in c. 480 B.C.

39

540

Bronze statuette of a woman holding a pigion in her right hand. Found on the mount Pindos and datable to c. 460 B.C.

Asklepios. Copy of the stat of Asklepios worshipped Athens in about 420 B.C.

129

Athena Parthenos the so-called "Varvakeion Athena" because it was found near the Varvakeion School.

Marble head of a woman, found in 1878, to the south of the Acropolis, near Dionysos' Theater.
The head, slightly reclining rested on her right arm, the traces of which are still visible on the right ear. It belonged probably to a statue of abandoned Ariadne. Above the dionysian ribbon encircling her head, she was wearing a diadem adorned by bronze rosaces. There were holes below the ears to attach it. A beautiful work ascribed to Skopas. Height 1 ft. 3., 4th century B. C. Cat.

The Ephebe of Anticythera. Bronze statue found in the sea off Anticythera in 1900. It may be the depiction of a god, hero or athlete. Made in c. 340 B.C.

The Ephebe of Anticythera (detail).

The head of Hygeia. Found at Tegea and probably made by Skopas in c. 360 B.C.

Marble statue of the goddess Themis. Found in the temple of Themis at Ramnous. Made in c. 280 B.C.

46

231

47

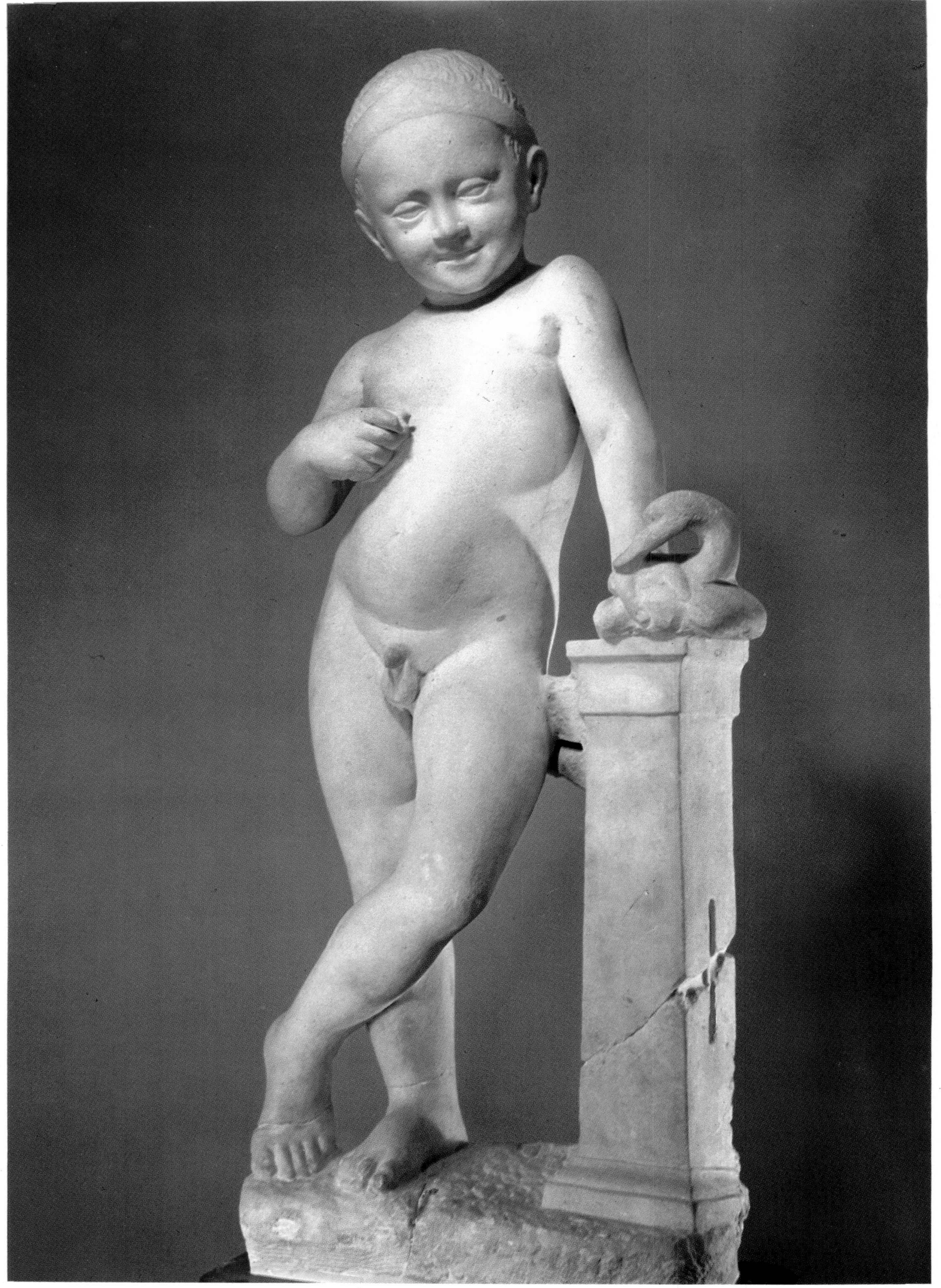

The Child with the Goose. Marble statuette found in the Kifissos river. Datable to the 3rd cent. B.C.

13400

48

Bronze head of the Philosopher of Anticythera found in the sea of Anticythera. Made in 240 B.C.

49

Bronze head of a boxer made by the sculptor Silanion between 335-330 B.C.

6439

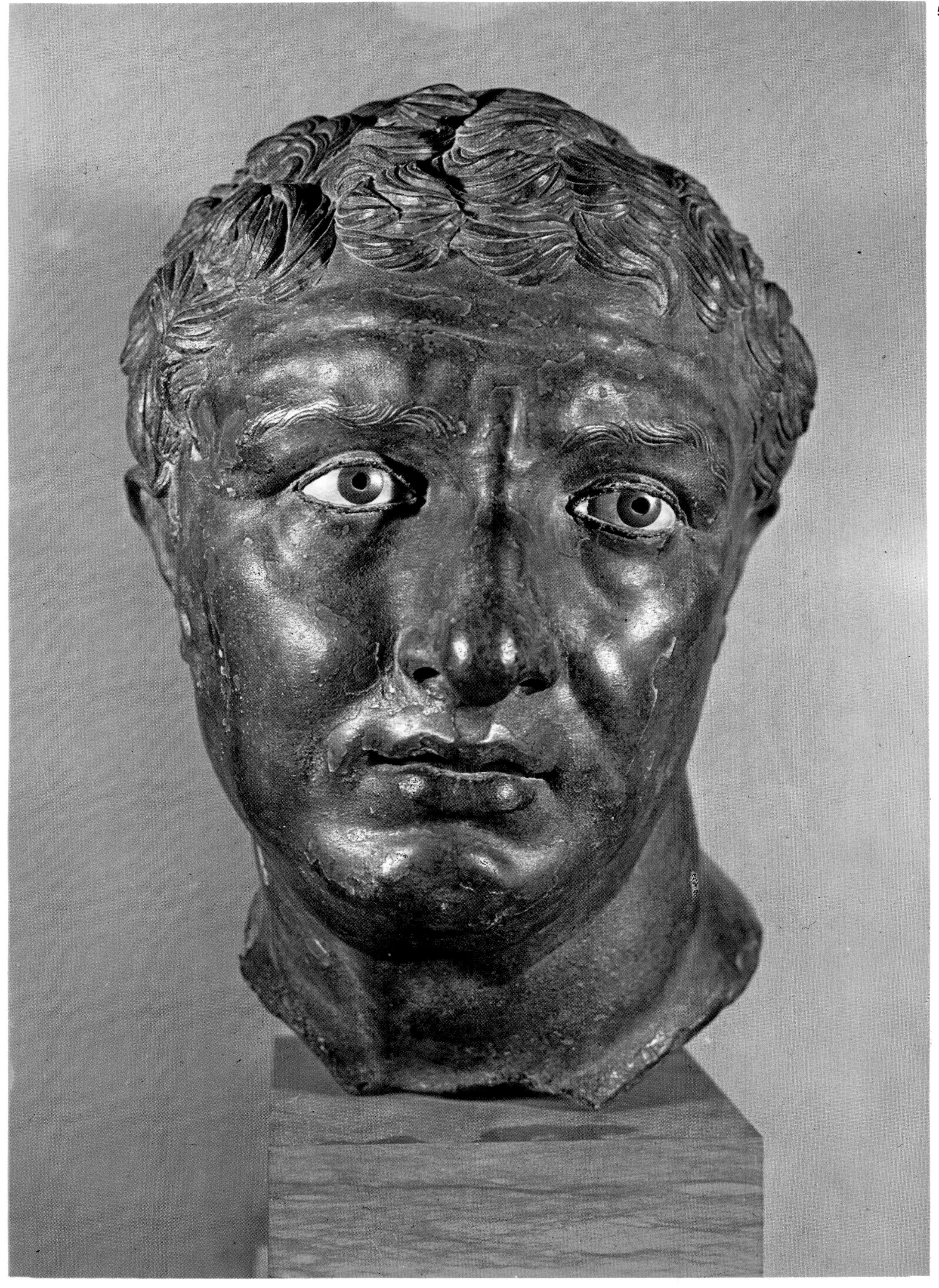

Brønze head of young man with strikingly vivid eyes. Found at Delos. Ist cent. B.C.

Colossal marble statue of Poseidon of Melos. 2nd cent. B.C.

51

235

5·2

Marble comic mask found near Dipylon. Made in the 2nd cent. B.C.

3335

53

The marble group of Aphrodite,
Pan and Eros. Ist cent. B.C.

54

Offering tables with wonderful presentations of a sea style. It comes from the excavations of Akrotiri at Thera. Dated c. 1500 B.C.

Ostrich egg transformed into a rhyton. The top, the handles and the base are of a greenish faience. From the excavations of Thera.

55

Three Theraic "kymbes" decorated with dolphins, lilies and swallows

1854

57

"Prochous" (vase) decorated with birds and reed-like presentations. From the excavations of Thera.

58

The Boxing Children. Fresco from the excavations at Thera. The artist has masterfully portrayed two children wearing gloves and engaged in boxing. The bodies are painted red, the hair is dark black, while the ears and the ankles of the children are ornamented with jewels. Made in c. 1550 B.C.

59

The fresco of the Boxing Children (detail).

Thera frescoes (detail).

60

62

Thera fresco from the House of the Ladies.

The fresco of the Spring from the excavations of Akrotiri, Thera. it covers the three walls of a room totally extending over 14 m². The fresco depicts a Theraic landscape before the volcanic eruption. Slender lilies grow among the multi-coloured rocks, while swallows flutter about in a state of intoxication. 1550-1500 B.C. 

63

The fresco of the Boxing Children. On the next wall of the same room th
fresco of the Antelopes. The animals' outlines are sketched by black line
against a whitish background. They come from the excavations of Ther
c. 1550 B.C.

64

65

The fresco of the Spring (detail).

66

Theraic fresco from the House of the Ladies. Probably a priestess.

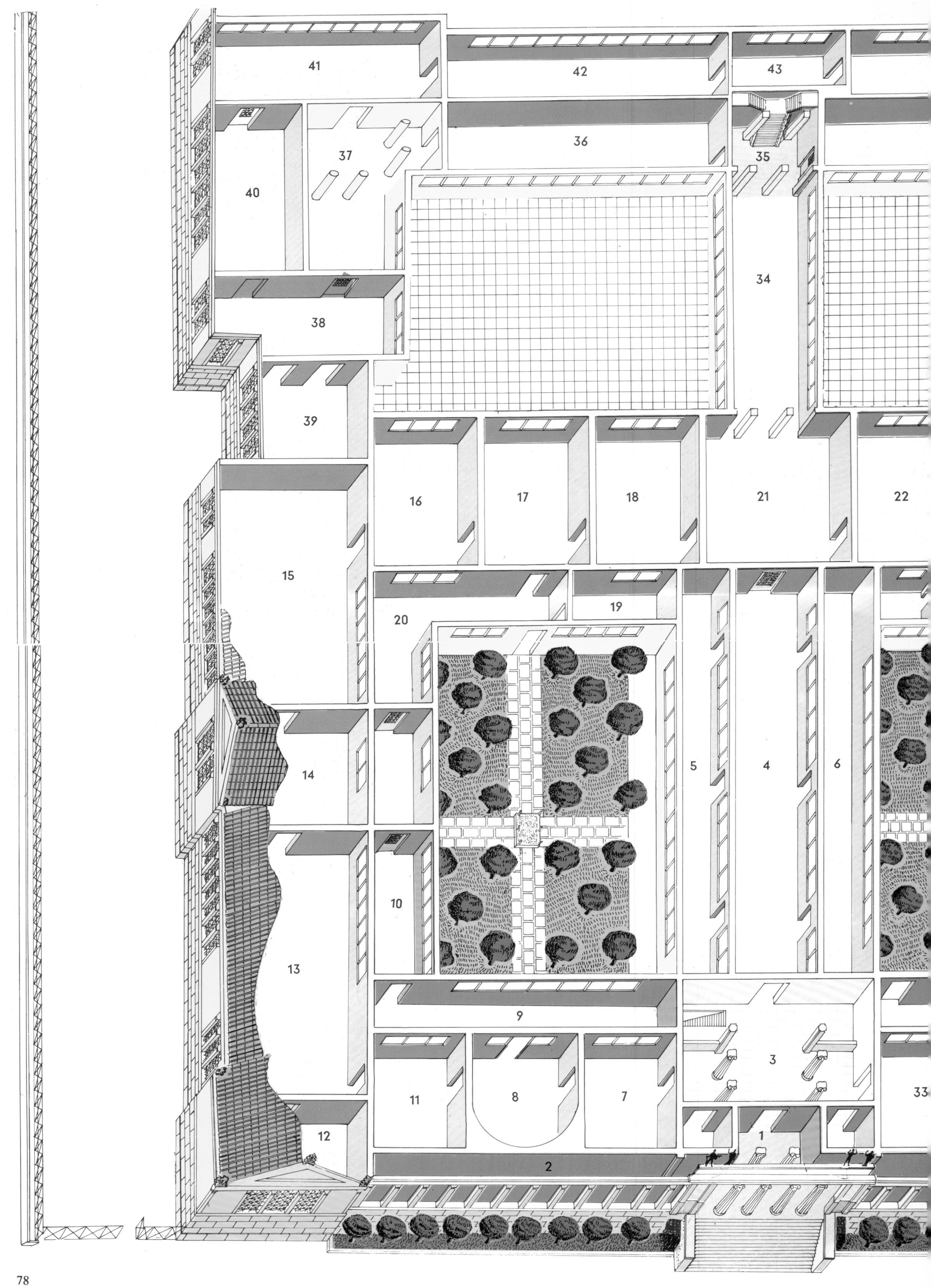
41
42
43
40
37
36
35
34
38
39
16
17
18
21
22
15
20
19
5
4
6
14
10
13
9
3
11
8
7
33
12
1
2

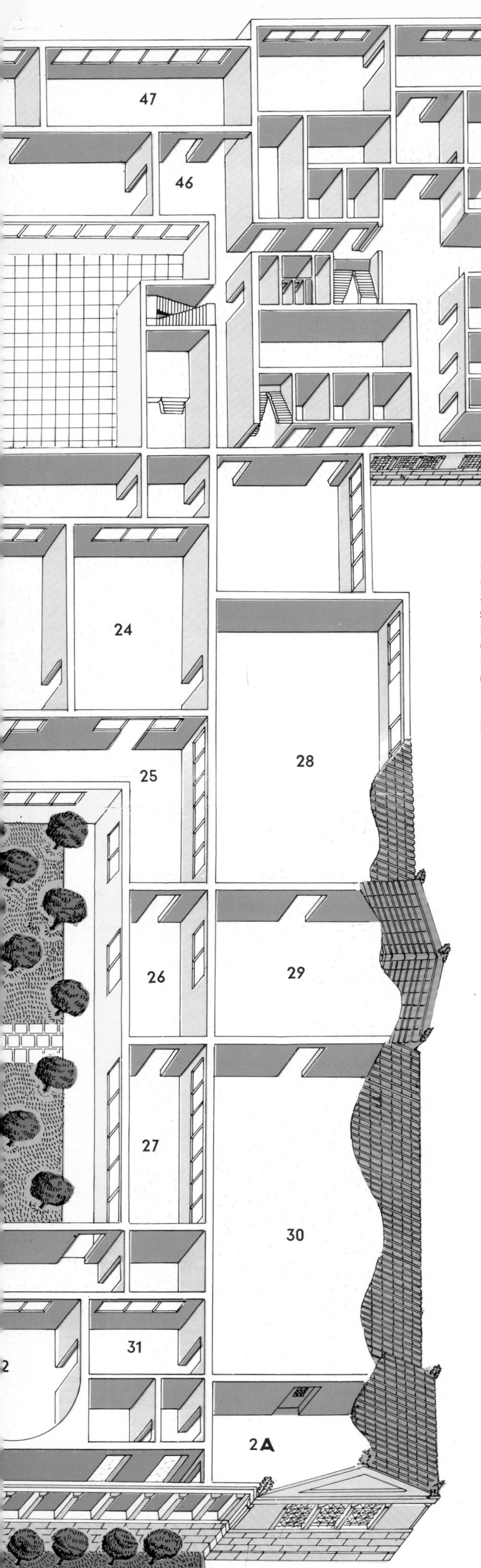

67

Plan of the National Archaeological Museum

1 Entrance 2A Exhibition of mouldings 3 Entrance-hall 4 Mycenaean hall 5 Neolithic finds 6 Cycladic finds 7-13 Archaic Art 14 Early 5th century 15 Early 5th century, Poseidon's hall 16-20 Classical Art, 5th century. Gravestone stelae and votive reliefs 21 Diadoumenos' hall 22 Sculptures from the sanctuary of Asclepios at Epidauros 23-24 Gravestone stelae, 4th century 25-27 Votive reliefs, 4th century 28 Youth of Anticythera's hall 29 Themis' room, 3rd century 30 Hellenistic Art 32 Stathatos Collection 34 Votive sculptures, hall leading to the new building of the Museum 35 Stairs to the upper floor. Ceramic collection 36 Carapanos Collection, Dodona 37 Bronze Collection 38-47 Rooms closed for rearrangement

Disposition of the statues and pieces of art in the various rooms of the Museum

Illustration page	Work No	Room No	Illustration page	Work No	Room No
1	3908	6	39	540	36
2	3909	6	40	263	43
3	624-253-259-254	4	41	129	20
5-6	1758-1759	4	42	-	28
7	395-765-394	4	43-44	13396	28
8	384	4	45	3602	28
9	4575	4	46	231	29
10	5878	4	47	2772	30
11	804	7	48	13400	30
12	2720	8	49	6439	30
13	29	11	50	14612	30
14	1558	9	51	235	30
15	21	9	52	3373	30
16-17	1906	10	53	3335	30
18	38	10	54	**Thera**	**room**
19	1959	12	55	1854	
20-21	15161	15	56	101-564-100	
22	126	15	57	1838	
23	715	16	58		
24	3624	18	59		
25-26	15177	21	60		
27	218	21	61		
28	1826	21	62		
29-30	15118	45	63		
31-32	—	45	64		
33-34	—	45	65		
35	6447	37	66		
36	16547	36	67		
37	6440	37	68		
38	6446	37			

NATIONAL ARCHAEOLOGICAL MUSEUM OF ATHENS